The **Essential**
Drinking Games
Book

D1311935

W a r n i n g :

This book is intended for the amusement of adults (you know who you are) who are of legal drinking age (ditto).

The author and Mud Puddle Books encourage you to drink (and play) responsibly and, in doing so, disclaim all liability for claims that arise out of uses (and abuses) of this book.

When using this book:

- **Do not drive!**
  Make certain that your designated driver is not a participant in your festivities.

- **Do not operate heavy machinery!**
  Rome wasn't built in a day because drinking game participants kept trying to build things.

- **Do not attempt sex!**
  Your partner will be greatly disappointed and you'll be humiliated beyond belief!

The
Essential
Drinking Games
Book

Chris Tait

Mud Puddle Books
NEW YORK

The Essential Drinking Games Book
By Chris Tait

© 2006 Chris Tait

Published by
Mud Puddle Books
54 W. 21st Street
Suite 601
New York, NY 10010
info@mudpuddlebooks.com

ISBN: 1-59412-130-3

Printed and bound in China

Contents

Chapter One

**(the sordid, honorable tradition and history of sport drinking
in which all things are begun with the best of intentions)**

*L*IKE ANY GUIDEBOOK worth it's salt, this one begins with a list of assumptions and exclusions.

It is widely assumed that if you are reading this guide and preparing to partake of libations, that you are legally and clinically permitted to do so.

It is also assumed that you are intending to drink competitively, but that this competitive spirit will be amateur in nature and so, more akin to the Olympic spirit than, say, your actual cockfight.

Now, my god, drinking games date back to pre-Dionysian times and are a final and honorable path to depravity. Lyndon Johnson himself once said that any man who couldn't play a few decent rounds of quarters ought to be flogged.*

In actual fact, the drinking game was played by the energetic youth of ancient Greece while at Symposia. And the Romans too, competitive in all things, played drinking games that included poetry, toasting and riddles.

---

*May not be at all factual. Editor.

Failure to finish a poem or answer a riddle would result in the punitive/rewarding drink we've all come to understand as central to the drinking game.

Dice games that encouraged rapid drinking were also popularized by the Roman youth. We shouldn't be too encouraged by this as they also invented the vomitorium.

And, while Cato and Caeser were moderates, as Rome began to slide, so did her behavior and that decline was led by Marc Antony and his raucous drinking binge games and parties.

The honest truth is that drinking games continued without change pretty much until the plague and the black death caused confused hordes of panic-stricken peasants to really step up their game and drink even more frantically in the hopes that these efforts might distill bad spirits. No real word yet on how that finished up.

If demolished civilizations, plagues and rampant peasants are no deterrent for you, then you, my friend, are in good company.

Read on and learn the sacred arts.

Chapter Two
(a discussion of the ground rules and how to get started during which the William Holden helmet is referenced)

*N*OW, FAR BE IT FOR ME to ask for thanks, pity or actual acknowledgement of injury endured, but it's worth noting that in the compilation of this tome, your guide made himself and, frankly, those around him, ill on numerous occasions.

Which is to say that the nature of all competition is that there must always be records kept and, of course, records broken. Always there is the subtle adjustment of the game, and, often, the hugging of the porcelain. Some things cannot be avoided and are better spoken of than dismissed. The ivory goddess and her worship fall into this nauseous category.

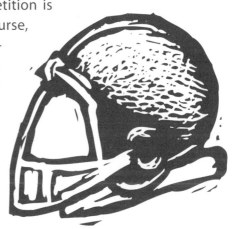

And so, while I cannot offer you the complimentary William Holden drinking helmet that was suggested, mocked up and rigorously tested in the original incarnation of this project, and which was only abandoned due to sheer size and shipping concerns, I can suggest that you take some precautions as you prepare yourself to shenanigan.

First, look around you. Are the crowd you are about to perform said drinking games with of sound character? Are they caring, considerate and conscientious? Are they in the pursuit of amusement and frivolity, of entertainment and enjoyment.

Or, have you, in all honesty, just committed yourself into the care of an evil and unknown brother/sisterhood of lechery and vice plottingly to render your person and, in all likelihood, their own, to misery and devolution?

Secondly, do you honestly have what it takes? This may be difficult to answer as you embark on your adventure. But I ask you as your guide to take a good hard look at yourself and make the most basic judgement call. Gaze into the abyss of your soul and at the man/woman/transgendered individual in front of you.

Are you the type who drinks blender beverages only with small umbrellas? Do you largely consider beer and it's copious consumption distasteful and vulgar? And, finally, are you really quite sure you're ready to put your personhood to the test in the face of braying inebriates and the horde of fools you've surrounded yourself with?

If you read the above and shrugged with incomprehension or nonchalance and grinned in a way that is decidedly lopsided, you are ready. Prepare to descend and to declare your supremacy in the arena of alcholic sportsmanship. Prepare to put dignity, sanity and decorum to bed with warm milk.

Let the games begin.

Chapter Three
(the dreaded Fuzzy Duck)

Danger: Immediate and present
Difficulty: Increasing
Focus required: Linguistic limber
Implements: More than three people, copious alcohol, possibly a table

*L*EAVE IT TO THE BRITISH to develop a game both ridiculously simple and devastatingly impossible to while away the hours and grey cells. Yes, it's the dreaded Fuzzy Duck. A game perfectly designed for getting to know the table around you. The starter of all starter drinking games.

For the unitiated, Fuzzy Duck is a game that will without variance result in what the natives call *getting plastered*. It will also have you cursing like a sailor on two-day shore leave, and, in all likelihood, snorting with laughter until beverages are projected from nostrils. If this sounds like your bag, carry on.

How it works:

Get the several people you have about you and decide on a starting Duck (all will be revealed, patience). Once you have determined said Duck, you will proceed in a clockwise fashion around the table. The Duck will say "Fuzzy Duck" to the person on their immediate left. This next person will say the same phrase and this will continue around the table. It is best if you do this all extremely quickly.

Now, here is where the change occurs. One of your herd will decide, at their discretion and without notice, to utter the phrase "Does he?" Quickly now, the direction of the tide changes to counter clockwise and each person must say "Ducky Fuzz." To change the tide, a person must only utter the phrase "Does he" and the pendulum once again swings.

Before you protest that this exercise seems ludicrously easy, I suggest that you put your skills to the test.

Any mistake in direction or in pronunciation results in a drink. Trust me when I say that bedlam is not far off. Here is an example of an actual Fuzzy Duck exchange:

Fuzzy Duck
Fuzzy Duck
Fuzzy Duck
Does He
Ducky Fuzz

Ducky Fuzz
Does He
F*ck, he does . . . ah f*ck!
Fuzzy Duck
Fuzzy Duck
Does he?
Does he f*ck . . . ah f*ck!

You see how this exchange will go. To add a layer of intrigue, insist that there be no repetitions of a phrase by any player within one round. In other words, if you have said Fuzzy Duck already in a session before an error, you may not say it again and may say only one of the other two phrases (Ducky Fuzz or Does he?). This is not as complex as it sounds. And, of course, should you botch this, you will be made/permitted to drink.

Finally, you may also allow your players to double up on Does He's. In other words, should someone attempt to change direction with a Does He, the next player can then say Does He and once again reverse the direction (provided this is their first Does He of the round.)

Does he recommend Fuzzy Duck?

*F*ck, he does!*

Chapter Four
(becoming a Quarters master)

Danger: Deceptively low
Difficulty: Surprisingly high
Focus required: Hand-eye coordination
Implements: More than three people, copious alcohol, table, a coin, a glass

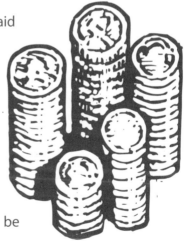

AH, QUARTERS. What can be said that hasn't been said by the poets of yesteryear? Who can forget the classic Socratic exchange documented in Plato's Republic referring to Quarters between Socrates and Adeimantus.

Quarters is a game designed by and for idiots.

Your aim is terrible and you are a miserable loser. Shut up and drink your mead.

Quarters is, in my estimation, one of the essential drinking games. A game that combines alcohol with projectiles, as our forefathers intended. A game to be played on a deserted island, on the deck of a swaying ship and in the most depraved of gin joints. You are destined to play this game at a kegger. You cannot shirk destiny. It knows where you live.

How it works:

Right! Here's how the boat floats. Assemble your crew around a table or, should there be no table, around a floor. It is assumed here that you can find the floor. If in doubt, lie down. There it is, your old friend floor.

Now, beginning with whomever you choose, place your cup, glass or bowl and place it in the center of the flat surface. Next, take your coin and attempt to bounce it off the table and into the receptacle.

If you succeed, you can tell any member of the table (or floor) to consume a pre-decided amount. This can be in sips or beers, depending on the level of professionalism and experience. You will also be awarded a second turn. Miss and the turn passes to the next player.

Should a player land three quarters in a row, they will gain the special privilege to make a rule.

This rule can be something as mundane as "whoever says beer, has to drink" to as complicated as "the first person to put their elbow on the table has to drink a shot".

Try, if you have it in you, to use your imagination. Of course, any violations result in drinking.

Slightly disgusting variations

Of course, wherever a cup is involved, there is the perfectly natural and understandable need to fill it.

There, in the center of your table, is a cup. Now, what if you were to fill it with, oh, I don't know, beer, or better still, something scotchy. Scotch perhaps.

Now, you have an enhanced version of quarters. Land your quarter in said glass and it becomes the glass to drink from. You could also create the condition that the glass must be devoured in one gulp (this is called chugging) and that the quarter must not be swallowed.

You could also play a version of quarters that includes "Rims." In this version, if you hit the rim of the glass, you are awarded a second chance at sinking the quarter. Sink your second shot and the game proceeds as per usual. Miss and you will be punished by having to drink the shot yourself. Cruel and poetic but appropriate.

Chapter Five

(The Icetray)

Danger: Impending
Difficulty: Self-inflicted
Focus required: Hand-eye coordination, possibly addition
Implements: More than three people, copious alcohol, possibly a table (floor as previously noted), icetray, coin

NOW, THE ICETRAY IS, at it's heart, simply a place where Quarters goes when it goes away to school.

Yes, it always remembers the place where it came from, with only a table and a coin as friends, but it's moved on. It's not going to go back? To do what, get some job in the feed mill? Settle down, get married and boom? No, the icetray has aspirations, amigo.

How it Works:

Take your same group of simian-types. Gather them around in a group and produce the coin. Now, you'll need to be in the kind of place where an icetray can be produced.

If you are going to be somewhere where there is none, you'll need to decide, in advance, to bring one.

That's not condescension, by the way, it's what guides do, it's called helping.

At any rate, once you have produced these conditions, you'll need a lot of beer and you'll need to put your ice-tray in the center of the table.

Now, here is where it gets a bit dangerous. As you can imagine, it is much easier to put a quarter into an icetray with a bounce than a glass. This is why you must make it challenging and painful.

Decide among yourselves which side of the icetray will be labeled Give. Land your quarter in this side of the tray and you will be awarded the power to give a drink to anyone in the group. This will be pleasant and joyful.

The other side of the tray will be labeled Take. You won't need to decide this as it will be the other side of give and your logic, as a group, will help you determine this without serious argument.

Mistakenly drop your quarter into this side and you will be punished by having to take a drink. Add this to the potential for others to award you a drink and you will understand the issues. Your hand-eye coordination will not, except in rare WKRP-type instances, improve.

To add another wrinkle, you may decide to use each pocket of the tray as a counting device. Land your quarter three holes away from you on the give side, and give three drinks. Land it three away on the take, and prepare to meet thy maker.

Chapter Six

(Captaining Caps)

Danger: Relatively low
Difficulty: Intermediate
Focus required: Hand-eye coordination, interpersonal skills
Implements: At least four people, beer in bottles

AH, MORE GAMES WITH BOOZE, airborne objects and opposition. Caps has the advantage of being a team game. Which means you'll have to choose your enemies, which is always nice. You'll also get to feel that sense of camaraderie in competition along with the solid opportunity for some real belching. In essence, though, in my esteemed opinion, Caps is really a game about talking sh*t about the other team and running them down at the mouth. And if that ain't a way to spend an afternoon, I don't know what is.

How It Works:

Line up your team against your opponents across the table or floor. Caps is a good game for places where you have nothing but a case of beer, like tailgate parties or camping trips.

Now, place an empty glass between the two teams. There will be some scoring, so be sure to save all of your caps as scoring implements. You could go so far as to add writing utensils and paper, but I think that's complicating a simple and beautiful thing.

Next, pick a team to start. Try to throw your cap, without bouncing, into the center glass. If you make it, you score a point. The other team must drink. If however, on their next turn, they score a point, your team has to drink and the point is scored for them but not for you. Unless, of course, you can answer that point with one of your own, in which case there is a lot of drinking and not much point recording. This continues until you have a miss.

This game can be played until 20 points or until you run out of beer. I think it's best to limit the score to 20 and then to switch teams.

Remember, the point of this game, other than the copious consumption of alcoholic beverages, is to really come up with as many insults and derogatory phrases as you can about the other team.

Anybody can throw a cap into a beer glass but only a true athlete can cause an entire room of drunken louts to yell "*Oh snap!*" with a single insult. It's not a game until someone loses an eye, folks.

Chapter Seven

(Three Man and Other Dicey Diversions)

Danger: Sneaking
Difficulty: Nil
Focus required: The good lady luck
Implements: At least three brave souls, libations, a pair of dice

THREE MAN IS A DICE GAME of the utmost quality. It's convoluted and, frankly, just weird. If you don't know, there's nothing better than a dice game for bringing out the bizarre in people. Whistling, kissing the dice, praying to the gods, yelling of lucky phrases, it's all on the table.

And, of course, once you master the numbers, you realize that this is really a game where everybody wins. This is assuming, of course, that winning is represented by ingestion of toxins and yelling of bizarre epithets in loose company, which, I assume, it is. Finally,

Three man has on it's side that it is a good game for those in a hurry to get where they are going. If they are going to Loopyland, this is the express bus.

How it Works:

Firstly, you will need to determine which of your clan will be the three man. This can be done by each of you taking a roll of the dice. The first of you to three is, you guessed it, the three man.

Is being the three man a good thing? You decide.

The player to the left of the three man goes first and play continues in a clockwise fashion.

Here's how the dice break down:

1 : 1   This is doubles. In doubles, the roller gives a single die to two people or two dice to one person. Whatever is rolled by those people/person is the number of drinks they must take.

1 : 2   Hey, these dice total three! That means the three man drinks. You'd be surprised how often this happens. Maybe you wouldn't.

1 : 3   This totals four! But wait, doesn't it *have* a three in it? Good enough for me. Three man, bottoms up.

1 : 4 Put your thumb to the table or cell floor. Don't get smart, whippersnapper. It doesn't have to make sense. It's the rules and rules rule. That's their job. You do your job and they'll do their job.

1 : 5 Put your index finger to the side of your nose and keep it there until your next turn. Don't ask any questions, just concentrate. Harder to do after ten minutes of playing than it sounds. Remove the finger, take a drink.

1 : 6 Relief! The player to your left must drink. This applies to all totals of seven.

2 : 2 And so, we return to doubles.

2 : 3 Another three. Three man is once again employed.

2 : 4 Incredibly, this is a pass. You and your table are spared. Next!

2 : 5 Ah, a total of seven. Player to the left drinks.

2 : 6 Another pass. Breathe deeply without intake of alcohol.

3 : 3 Doubles. *Capiche?*

3 : 4 Why, it's our old friend three. Three man?

3 : 5   Also threeing. Poor three man. He seemed so smart only moments before.

3 : 6   Ah, this is better, a social. Raise your glasses all!

4 : 4   Doubles. Nuff said.

4 : 5   Sociable.

4 : 6   Pass

5 : 5   Honestly, you get this part, right?

5 : 6   Player to the right of roller drinks. This applies to all 11s. Of which there are exactly this one.

6 : 6   I'm not explaining this part anymore.

So, here's where the Three man's life is spared. Should the three man roll a three or a combination of dice that add up to three (of which, again, there is only one), he is no longer the three man. Better still, he/she gets to designate the three man. In addition, if the three man is made to roll on a double and rolls a three or a combination that adds up to three, the same rule applies and they are spared.

It's not really that complex. Here's the Cliff notes:

Doubles: Give the dice away

Any three or sum of three: Pity the three man, for he will drink

Total of Seven: Player to the right drinks

Total of Eleven: Player to the left drinks

Total of nine: Social, everybody drinks.

One and four: Thumb on floor/table

One and Five: Finger on the side of the nose, Kringle!

Chapter Eight

(The Classic: Zoom, Schwartz, Pafigliano)

Danger: Low
Difficulty: Complex for the kisser
Focus required: Clear pointing ability required
Implements: More than three people, hooch, index fingers

WINNER OF THE MOST RIDICULOUSLY Named Drinking Game six years running, Zoom, Schwartz, Pafigliano remains one of the essential drinking games. I learned to play this gem when I was but a boy, drinking from some friends' absent parents' liquor cabinet a concoction we used to call swamp juice. Should you have the desire to recreate these conditions, simply combine two ounces of everything in your liquor cabinet into a large juice jug and begin playing Zoom, Schwartz, Pafigliano. I assure you the results will be hideous.

It's the kind of game that was created in the mists of time but that endures due to it's simple charm and it's endearing features of both pointing and yelling.

How it works:

There are only four words required in Zoom, Schwartz, Pafigliano which makes it perfect for ESL clubs. These words are Zoom, Schwartz and yes, Pafigliano. You will begin the game using the fourth word, which is GO! You will also have cause to say Zoom backwards, which will sound like the plural of a noise a cow makes: Mooz.

Here's how to make use of them.

First, one person turns to his neighbor and shouts GO! The next person points to anyone else in the circle and says either Zoom, Mooz, Schwartz or Pafigliano.

Zoom puts the focus on the pointed at.

Mooz passes focus directly to the right of the pointed at.

Schwartz also passes focus to the pointed at.

Pafigliano passes focus to who had the focus last, regardless of where the pointer is pointing.

Now, I can see you saying to yourself, aren't Zoom and Schwartz the same, my illustrious guide?

Yes, but there is an additional rule.

You cannot Pafigliano after a Schwartz.

You also may not Schwartz three times in a row.

Break any of these rules, or worse, take too long to figure out your move, and you will be drinking. At which point, start over by yelling GO!

Essential to this game are the keeping up of pace, yelling volume and clarity and, of course, the proper obnoxious gusto when pointing.

I guarantee you that this game will make you instant friends with all those in the room regardless of language ability, as you will all be behaving like frothing inmates within five minutes and all delusions of civility and social nicety will be but memories.

Chapter Nine
(Building the Beeramids)

Danger: Dependant on participants
Difficulty: Moderate complexity
Focus required: Some shuffling ability, brief periods of memory work
Implements: More than three people, firewater, a full deck of cards

BEERAMIDS IS ALSO sometimes called Beer Bullshit. I like the name Beeramids as it makes me think not only of the great beermakers of ancient times and their fine tombs but also the happy days when I have been amid beers.

Beeramids is a dangerous game, but it is entirely dependant on the level of competitiveness among your tribe. A relatively benign game of Beeramids is there for the taking but for the love of all that is hoppy and holy, set the standard high and challenge often.

How it Works:

Commence the build. First off, the dealer shuffles the cards and begins by dealing five rows of cards onto the table, face down. These will be the levels of your beeramid. The first of these gets one card, the second two and so on. You see how the stack is created. Each of these rows has a drink value against it. The stack with the five cards has a value of one drink, the row with four cards has a value of two drinks, three cards three drinks, four cards two drinks and the final row, with one card, has a value of five drinks.

To begin, the dealer flips over one card in the five card pile. The first player may then pass or challenge another player. Pass is just that. Pass.

For a challenge, the player may choose a player and tell them that they have to drink the appropriate number of drinks for that row. This is based on the assumption that the challenging player has a match in his/her hand for the card that is face up.

The challenged player has two options. They may agree to the challenge and drink the amount, or they may counterchallenge, calling bullshit or, sometimes, f*ck off, depending on the hour of the night.

If the challenger has the card, the challenged must drink

double the amount originally challenged. If they do not, the challenger must drink double the amount.

You see where this leads. Much shouting and profanity and, by the time the beeramids have been built, no player is left unscathed. I urge you again, with great prejudice, to challenge early and often and to build your beeramids high and to build them wide. The eyes of the ancients are upon you.

Chapter Ten
(Shots and Spoons)

Danger: Possible risk of dislocation, scratching, clawing.
Difficulty: Rudimentary
Focus required: Hand-eye
Implements: More than three people, *beaucoup* booze,
a deck of cards, a goodly serving of spoons, table

I KNOW THAT MURRAY HEAD was speaking of chess when he declared his game "the ultimate test of cerebral fitness" but I for one prefer Shots and Spoons. For me, it has more spooniness and more centrally located shots as part of it's core strategy. I appreciate its candor and it's wit. I also like the way it leads to pawing, slapping and general bedlam.

How it Works:

Shots and spoons is like musical chairs for rummies, really. Now, the idea here is that there is one less spoon than people. Instead of music, however, you have cards.

Deal each player seven cards. Set the spoons in the middle of the table in a formation that you find pleasing. Star shape works to democratically give everyone a good shot at grabbing for them when the times comes.

The goal here is to get four of a kind and then to make your grab for your spoon. Obviously, the goal is to get the four of a kind, and failing this, to at the very least get yourself a spoon.

The dealer begins by picking the top card off of the deck. He then hands a card from his hand to the person next to him who hands a card to the person next to him. This is all meant to happen quickly and sloppily. It's not meant to be tidy and quiet. This continues until someone gets four of a kind. At which point they may lunge for, or, for the expert player, subtly slide a spoon off the table.

It is up to the other players to notice that a spoon has gone missing and to secure themselves one. This will involve much clutching and grabbing. The person who doesn't get a spoon, gets the titular shot.

Now, it is imperative that the person who started the

spoon grabbing be able to produce their four of a kind. If they can't, and this happens as things get later, they must take two shots.

In advanced play, you may introduce the fake. In the fake, you feign to grab a spoon without in fact touching a spoon. This will set off a flurry of activity and spoon grabbing and yelling. At first, you will be made to feel the loser but you will be vindicated. As cards are revealed, it will be seen that there are no four of a kinds and that the player who first spooned in fact did so in error. Two shots to them. Kudos to you.

You may also allow the winner of each hand to invent a ridiculous rule with consequences in the time-honored drinking game tradition.

Should the winner of a hand have more than seven cards in their hand when they declare themselves champion, they will, of course, be made to drink.

This game may also be played with beer but it's just not quite the same, is it?

Chapter Eleven
(Philly is for Fools)

Danger: Skulking
Difficulty: Nil
Focus required: Mild
Implements: More than just you, a deck of cards, a spare liver

AH, PHILLY. This is a game that I honestly believe was created by sailors who I imagine convalescing in a head-injury unit. The thing about Philly is it's unpretentious, you know? It knows who it is. It's not even going to try to be showy or complicated or, for that matter, particularly smart. This is the game that says, hey, who's kidding who, ya big palooka? I know what I'm doing here and I don't have, oh, say an hour to get this thing fired up.

How It Works:

Sit across from at least one person. Take a deck of cards and flip over the top one. Now, things get difficult, right? No, things get dumb. One of you decides if the next card is going to be higher or lower. Keep in mind that aces are wild.

If it's your turn, and you say lower, and tis indeed lower, you keep going. Lucky you. You can pass, but only after you've played down three cards. You get it wrong, you start again. Doesn't sound so bad. Oh, did I mention that if you are wrong, you have to drink however many cards are down in that pile? Yes, you do, lumpy.

So, here's what you'll want to do. Get to three. Pass! For the love of your own sanity, just pass. Pass! Oh, why don't you pass?

If you get the same number, say a four, then you start a new pile. You can obviously do this if you also get an ace.

Now, if you get your over/under wrong on your second pile, you have to drink twice the number of cards that are down.

On the third pile, if you have an error, you drink . . . yes, three times as many.

The game continues thusly until you run out of cards. And then you start again. If you get that far. But honestly, who's going to get that far? Philly is a game with a mission, my friend. And you are in its sights.

Chapter Twelve

(Spinners and Rims)

Danger: Mild
Difficulty: Varied
Focus required: Hand-eye
Implements: *Compadres*, cocktails and coins

*S*PINNERS AND RIMS ARE, for the purposes of this wee tome, grouped together as together they share a hip hop moniker, and the requirement of a coin. They're both good opening games and they are only mildly dangerous. So, whether you're using hydraulics on your pimped-out ride or you're just looking to get your drink on, these are the games for you. Read on, Macduff.

How They Works

How they works is that they both need you to get some *hombres* around a table with some fine beverages. (Martinis aren't going to be good as you're going to be slurping them, so I would lower the bar. Perhaps Lowenbrau?*)

Now, in the case of Spinners, the idea is that after everybody has poured themselves a frosty friend, the first of you is going to put a quarter on edge and flick it with your index finger so that it careens with great force around the table.

While she spins, you're going to call out the name of someone sitting at the table. They then have two options:

First, they can stop the quarter from spinning by placing their finger on the top, halting it, ever so daintily, on its edge. This is, as you can imagine, extremely difficult. Should the quarter fall over, or should the attempt fail, they will, of course, down their entire beverage.

They have a further option. They may also line up the quarter while it still spins and flick it themselves, sending it spinning again. They will then call out another name and that person will have the opportunity to flick the quarter themselves to send it spinning.

Should any of these spinners knock the quarter off of the table or should the quarter fall flat on the table (don't worry big boy, it happens), the spinner will partake of the punitive drink.

It's an easy game, but it's friendly and involves flicking and firing coins at each other, and, dammit, I like it.

---

*Profuse apologies. Editor .

Rims or Rimmers, as some call it, is a game that lets you fire coins at each other and have a good time doing it. For this game, I recommend the sturdy, tiny and bite-sized American dime. Dimes are small enough to bounce quite nicely without a helluva lot of force, which is what you want here.

To rim properly, you must sit about with your amigos and, in a clockwise fashion, each take aim bouncing your dime off of the table. The goal is to land your little ten-cent piece directly in the glass of your target. Success, they drink. Now, it's not called Rims for nothing.

Hit the edge of the glass (which will give you a satisfying pinging noise) and you yourself, as the bouncer, must quaff.

There is some salvation to be had in the knowledge that if you miss the glass entirely, your turn is simply passed.

It's fast, it's fun, there is that good crossbar noise and there is some chuckling to be had in throwing objects at each other, as I have detailed in some . . . detail, previously.

Chapter Thirteen
(The Beer Hunter)

Danger: Watch the eyes!
Difficulty: Subhuman
Focus required: Sorry, what?
Implements: Beer, possibly beer goggles

*N*OW, EVEN THE MOST CASUAL couch potato should be aware that the beer hunter was popularized on television by the budget comic geniuses at SCTV.

If you haven't seen Bob and Doug MacKenzie, two "hoser" characters created by Doug Thomas and Rick Moranis in action, find your way to a clip online or a dvd store. You can rent them or, better yet, get yourself a genuine copy of the Bob and Doug McKenzie album Great White North or the film Strange Brew. The film is a bizarre take on Hamlet that has to be seen to be

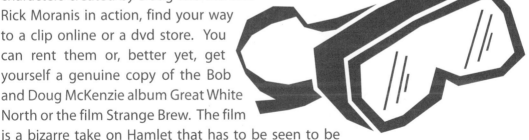

believed. Max Von Sidow and Mel Blanc contribute their talents and, well, it's filmed in hose-a-rama, so it has to be good.

How It Works

To say that the Beer Hunter lacks complexity is to say that Clinton was a little loose with the ladies.

Make no mistake about it, the Beer Hunter is, as Bugs would say, mud spelled backwards.

But that don't mean she can't be a riot.

Here's how to play. Get yourself a case of beer. Hell, get two. Now, my best approach would be to get yourself a six pack and put it between you and your friend. One of you close your eyes. The other of you reach down and pull out one of the beers.

Take that beer and shake it. Don't just shake it a little. I mean, really, really shake the hell out of it.

Shake it like it owes you money.

Now, put it back in the box. Next up, you close your eyes. Your friend reaches in and shuffles the beers around and they now take out a beer and perform the same operation.

Here's where the fun begins. The first of you takes out a beer, points it at your head on an angle (I kid you not) and opens it. Should it fire out a foamy lather at your head with great force, there is great mirth to be had. Should it not, drink your beer with great speed and your turn, she is finished without serious injury. You see where this goes.

At some point in the next 12 minutes, someone is going to get a headfull of beer. I'd like to claim that there is a great building of intrigue in this game, but really, it's just waiting for the money shot, isnt' it? But don't worry, the wait, she is short.

Enjoy and don't forget to wear your goggles kids!

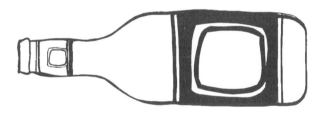

Chapter Fourteen
(Ibble Dibble)

Danger: Mostly cosmetic
Difficulty: Mild
Focus required: You're going to need to pay some attention, yes
Implements: Beer, folks, tables and some form of marking device

IBBLE DIBBLE IS ONE of those quick little games that you decide to play and then one of you regrets all night long having made that decision. I like it because it combines competition with humiliation, mocking and catcalling, like all great societal rituals.

Here's How It Works:

Everyone around your table gets together to have at least one drink. Next up, you're going to number everyone who is there. You're going to need the aforementioned marking device which can either be a) a marker, b) the classic charred cork or, really, anything that's nice and smudgy.

Just for your home-scoring kit: an IBBLE DIBBLE is a soon-to-be-saucy player of said game. DIBBLE IBBLE is the mark made on the player by the marker.

Here's what y'all do. You must speak in quick cadence without pausing and you must continue to move at a great pace at all times. This is the edict, my friends.

Player one:

This is the #1 ibble dibble with no dibble-ibbles calling the #3 ibble-dibble with no dibble-ibbles.

Player Three:

This is the #3 ibble dibble with no dibble-ibbles calling the #4 ibble-dibble with no dibble-ibbles.

Basically, it's impossible to do this. I'm sorry to be the one to tell you, but it is.

When you do make your mistake, you will have to quaff a big swig and, importantly, you will be given your first IBBLE IBBLE.

Now, this mark will likely start off as being just a small stroke of color but will end up being either a full-on Little Rascals Petey eye or a gay caballero moustache. Either way, you're going to look good.

Now, you continue:

This is (fill in the number you are) with one dibble ibble calling the #5 ibble-dibble with no dibble-ibbles.

That ibble dibble must respond in kind and, as you progressively deteriorate, must somehow recall exactly how many marks he has on his face while knowing the other players numbers without counting them while he/she speaks.

Again, this is impossible. But that doesn't mean you can't try until you are nicely besmirtched and ready to head out for the night. The best element of Ibble Dibble, in my personal opinion, is that when you do head out, it's nearly impossible to lose your mates. Unless, of course, you run into a rival gang of dibblers. At which point, might I suggest a dance-off.

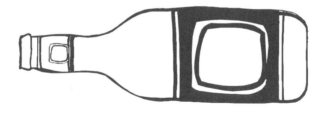

Chapter Fifteen

(The Dreaded Depth Charge)

Danger: Moderate
Difficulty: Acceptable
Focus required: Menial
Implements: Beer, boys, a pitcher, a glass

DEPTH CHARGE IS A GAME that your author enjoys very much. It has booze, it has big jugs, it has . . . I'm sorry, I can't go through with that. Honestly, it's a great game because you get to yell and scream and wait for the worst to happen as that little glass sinks lower and lower, sealing your doom!

How It Works:

Depth charge is not a complicated pastime, but it does require some talent and foresight. Essentially, what you're going to do is to to float a pint glass of beer in a pitcher of beer. Ah, beer in beer, what will they think of next?

Now, you're probably going to need to put a little beer in the bottom of the floating glass just to make it float nice and evenly. Once you've achieved this delicate balance, you're ready to play depth charge!

Each player in turn is going to pour an amount of beer into the floating pint glass. Some just slurp a little in there, some dump in a big swig of ye ole suds. Really, it's your call. But be warned. Be the one to sink the pint and you will be the one to reach into a soupy pitcher of beer and pull out a full pint and chug it.

The best element of this game is the opportunity to bellow the following: "She's going down! She's going down, ya big son of a bitch! (You may substitute any number of insulting epithets here.)

You might want to back this up with a bunch of back-slapping and also with a brief discussion of the shape of the surface of your pitcher of beer. That's right big boy, get ready to talk meniscus . . . or possibly minisci!

If you want to be especially clever, you can discuss the Archimedes principle, talk at great depth about displacement theory and so on and so forth. My bet is you will instead be chugging sloppy pints, and, quite possibly, belching. But one always holds out hope for the philistines.

Chapter Sixteen

(All Thumbs on Deck)

Danger: Fair to middling
Difficulty: Pay attention
Focus required: What are you new? Pay attention!
Implements: Beer, table, opposable digits

ALL THUMBS ON DECK is a game that is, quite frankly, for sports teams. I've seen it played by those who don't play sports and it's sad. I don't know why that is. Perhaps they are too artistic. Perhaps they are too evolved. My best guess is that they just can't handle the repetition. But really, all this game takes is a little paying attention and, frankly, thumbs.

Here's how it works:

Honestly, when I explain this game to people, they often stare at me, blink a few times and then shake their head. I know what they're thinking. They're thinking there should be more to it. That there should be some sort of evolution. But that's not what this game is for.

I was introduced to All Thumbs on Deck by a hockey team who play it every Monday night and have done so for over five years. Nothing ever changes and it's still as funny and still ends up with one really, really drunk guy and several half cut ones to boot.

First up, you don't tell anyone you're going to play ATOD. You just start. At some unforeseen point in a conversation, one of your group must nonchalantly place his thumb on the table, as discreetly as possible, pad down.

Now, this will have no affect for several minutes. But someone will catch the eye of the first in at some point and the first in will waggle his eyebrows or look downwards and soon this second in will slowly place his thumb on the table.

At this point, others may start to catch on rapidly and there will, without doubt, be a frenzy of thumbs slapping down on the table and a bunch of groaning.

Next up, you get to argue about who was last. Often, this is no contest as there is one guy or girl who is usually completely out to lunch in every crowd. They will often have to suffer, but that, as they say, is life.

But if it is close, there is a lot of "no way's" and "Freddy was totally last" and so on's. Honestly, it sounds really, really stupid, but it's good times for the whole team. You might need to pick up a sport first, that's my only caveat.

Chapter Seventeen

(The Evil of Cardinal Puff)

Danger: Severe
Difficulty: High
Focus required: Intense
Implements: More of your brain than you've used for a drinking game in a while, booze, plastic cups

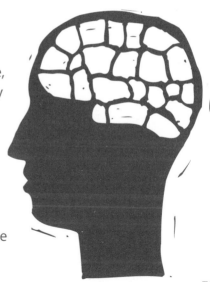

CARDINAL PUFF IS A GAME that I love because, frankly, it's needlessly cruel and ridiculously hard to play for even ten seconds without having to drink. I know no one who can play it properly and I know lots who play it often. So that tells ya something, don't it? Don't it?

How It Works:

Get yourself four to six of your pals and sit in a nice circle, preferably with some plastic cups.

Let's say you are the first to play. You shall do the following, my recruit.

Say, with your pinky finger extended, holding your drink with only your index finger and thumb: "I would like to drink to Carinal Puff for the first time tonight."

Then, with your index finger only, swipe across your eyebrow ONE time, one time across one side of your upper lip (as if drawing half of an imaginary moustache) and then across the other side one time. Now, tap the top of your lap on one side once and then the other side once. Next, stomp one foot and then the other.

Stand up and then, sit down. Do it again, repeating everything twice, saying "I would like to drink to Cardinal Puff for the second time tonight." Finally, do it one last time, saying, "I would like to drink to Cardinal Puff for the third and final time tonight." Now, do everything three times.

Finally, finish the cup, turn it upside down on the table and tap it there three times.

Of course, everyone else's job is to make sure that you don't make any mistakes. Make a mistake, any mistake, mind you, you finish your entire drink and have to wait until it returns to your turn, at which point, you will try again.

In the meantime, the turn passes and everyone tries to complete this seemingly simple exercise.

This is a very, very dangerous game. First off, you're trying to do something repetitive and complex and if you don't nail it the first time, and almost no one ever does, the surrounding distractions and conditions worsen and become more complicated. Miss a couple times and you will notice that you are on an island with the Cardinal and there may be no return to civilization. If you're going to play this game, start early in the day (noon is always nice) and set some kind of limit.

I'm telling you, the Cardinal, he takes no prisoners. Consider yourself warned.

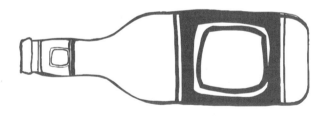

Chapter Eighteen

(Six Cups)

Danger: Dependant on luck
Difficulty: High
Focus required: Almost none
Implements: Four to six people, six cups, beer, horseshoes optional

SIX CUPS IS A LOVERLY LITTLE DICE GAME that requires mild concentration and allows you to flirt with the gods a little. Playing any game that requires only luck, you know you're going to hear from kharma at some point. Roll the dice and see how well you're loved by the immortals, why don't ya? It's only beer, what harm can it do?

How it Works:

You'll need four folks to play 6 cups well. The first team player rolls your one die and, should it come up, say, a 4, he/she has to fill the cup with beer that you've set up to match that number.

So, cup 4 is now filled with frothy goodness.

The next player now has the opportunity to roll their die. If it comes up a 4, they have to quaff from cup 4 and drain that cup with enthusiasm right to the last drop. I love a game with a goal!

Should they roll another number, a 5 perchance, they have to fill the 5 cup with beery bliss. You see how we're quickly running out of empty glasses.

The deadly part about this game is that the player must continue to play until they find a cup they can fill. This sounds easy, but should your turn fall after a few people have managed to hit different numbers, you could be in a spot. There is no definitive end to 6 cups that I know of, other than time running out or some poor sot crying uncle.

You don't want to get on the wrong end of a 6 cup run here, if you can avoid it. Trust me, it's a dicey proposition and you will feel the pain. Luck, be a lady tonight!

Chapter Nineteen
(Electric Jesus)

Danger: Dependant on luck
Difficulty: High
Focus required: Intense
Implements: From two to ten folk, booze, the trusty deck of cards

IF YOU'VE SEEN THE BIG LEBOWSKI, you know that no one fucks with the Jesus. But if you haven't, or you simply want to tempt the Jesus, this is your game. It should however, be noted that neither the author nor any sources consulted had any explanation for the title of the game. It doesn't make any damn sense, but that doesn't make it any less wonderful.

How It Works:

Get your crowd into the proverbial circle and deal each reprobate five cards. The rest of the deck you can stack into the center of the table.

Draw one card from the deck and place it face up on the table. This will be the "take one" card.

Should this card match your card, you must take one. Should this card be one that you have more than one of, you must take more than one. It's unfortunate, I know, but math was never really your friend.

The next card turned over will be the give card. Anyone possessing this card will be enabled to, in fact, give a drink.

It's lovely, really and you are welcome to pick on whomever you choose and to abuse your privelages. It wouldn't be a free country if you couldn't.

With larger groups of say eight to ten participants, to vary the game and to ensure projectile vomiting, try making this game work with only suits.

In other words, should you turn over a spade, all with spades must drink. The next card that is turned over, should it be a heart, all with hearts may award one drink. This is a lethal version of the game, suitable for playing when time is of the essence: last-call, death row, that kind of thing.

Chapter Twenty

(Twenty-one Aces)

Danger: Optional
Difficulty: Low
Focus required: Low
Implements: Five dice, a commercial bar, bartender, legal tender, tablemates

TWENTY-ONE, DESPITE IT'S CARD-LIKE NAME, is actually a dice game. It's a great game for playing in public places as it soon gathers a crowd and really, who doesn't want an audience for their inevitable inebriation?

How It Works:

Twenty-one Aces is simple to play and simple to follow and again, as a dice game, you either has the luck or you does not has the luck.

There is some strategy, but it's nominal at best. Mostly, it's the cojones, ya know?

To play, you'll need five dice. You play the game by counting only the ones that are rolled. Basically, you play by each taking a roll of the dice. The first of you rolls all of the dice. If you roll a one or more than one, pass along the remaining dice.

Continue this way until you get to the seventh one. The person who rolls this die gets to pick the shot you're going to order. Evil doers will always choose tequila but I myself dread even more the cream-based liqueur shot. It's just not straight pool.

Now, the person who rolls the fourteenth ace, is up on deck to pay for the shot. So, there's some pleasure in being seventh and some pain in being fourteenth. And, of course, whomsoever should roll the twenty first ace shall be the drinker of said shot.

It's also best to reduce the number of dice at certain intervals so that when the game resolves, there is some dramatic tension in the twenty first shot.

Par exemple, when you get to the 16th, remove one die and at each ace after, remove another. By the time you reach 20, you will be playing with only one die and there will be room for catcalling and yelling and so on and so forth.

Of course, in more serious company, the entire group will drink a shot, the fourteenth ace roller shall pay for the round and the twenty first ace roller shall simply double up.

Personally, this is the version I think is more suiting and my view is shared by numerous ex-cons and merchant marines, so I'm not alone.

Chapter Twenty-One

(Peuchre)

Danger: Massive
Difficulty: Medium
Focus required: Must know how to play Euchre
Implements: Five dice, a commercial bar, bartender, legal tender, tablemates

NOW, I CONSIDER THIS SECTION to be my own personal public service announcement. Think of it as my gift to you and heed my words heavily. There are a million games like this and, while you'll have noticed I recommended some games that have a high boozy level, this is a game that is beyond the pale.

There are many games like it and they are all to be avoided on pain of death. I'll show you how peuchre works, but more in the way that a jedi master might explain the dark side to a young one. You should know it's there but fer chrissakes, run for the hills . . .

How it Works:

Basically, peuchre is euchre where each point has a punishing drink attached to it. If you don't know how to play euchre, you should. What are you, five? All adults know how to play euchre.

So, basically, the point system is awarded thusly. Should you lose a point in a hand, you will take one drink per point. Now, if you do know euchre, you know this is not wise. You can easily end up with a couple of points against you every two minutes.

Should you get euchred, you shall consume five drinks for the euchre, plus drinks for each point.

Should your opponents take all tricks during a lone hand, you shall also drink ten drinks, plus points.

If your partner overtrumps you when he doesn't have to, your partner has to have two drinks.

If you are found to have reneged (card term meaning playing out of suit) you shall chug your entire pint in one slug.

Again, if you know how euchre works and the speed with which those who play it play it, you know this game is just, well, it's for the brave at liver.

In Contusion

FINALLY, AS YOUR GUIDE, it is my sincere wish that there be only mirth and happiness at the drinking table. But that's not really what the gang's after, are they? In all honesty, drinking games are designed to by and for consumption athletes, adrenalin junkies and ne'er do wells. But if you've made it this far, you're probably one of the above. If you weren't, you'd be sipping a vodka martini with a babe in some suave lounge. That may be you someday, but for now, beer helmets on! Who is more fool, the fool or the fool who . . . oh forget it . . .